CHRIST and the Powers

By Hendrik Berkhof

Translated from the Dutch
by John H. Yoder

HERALD PRESS
Scottdale, Pennsyl
Kitchener, Ontario

The original edition of this book was published in 1953 in Dutch under the title *Christus en de Machten*, by G. F. Callenbach N. V. of Nijkerk, The Netherlands.

CHRIST AND THE POWERS

Released simultaneously in Canada by Herald Press, Kitchener, Ont. N2G 4M5
Library of Congress Catalog Card Number: 62-13713
International Standard Book Number: 0-8361-1820-0
Printed in the United States of America.
Design: Alice B. Shetler

10 9 8 7 6 5

Contents

Translator's Preface

Few realms of biblical thought have until very recent years been so resolutely ignored by the main streams of Protestant theology as that which provides the theme of this booklet. For an age which no longer believed in spooks or in Santa Claus, there was something embarrassing about the way in which the Bible—and especially the Apostle Paul—spoke of the "Powers," that is, of some sort of undefinable superterrestrial beings, not only as if they existed, but in fact as if they mattered and were somehow involved in the work of Christ.

Not knowing what to do with the whole problem, it was easiest simply to set it aside as out-of-date. Then one was free to develop a philosophy of history, a view of the state, and a theology of culture according to one's own tastes and leanings, unhampered by the irrelevance of what looked like rabbinic metaphysics or apocalyptic angelology. Since what the Bible seemed to be saying seemed irrelevant, this freedom from the form of Paul's thought seemed to promise great strides forward. Yet somehow over the years the expected growing clarity of an up-to-date, yet Christian world view, capable of understanding the state and the structuredness of culture, yet without overvaluing them, has not come into focus. Too modern to think with Paul, we're not sure what to think at all.

Professor H. Berkhof has had the audacity—or the simple faith—to begin with the opposite assumption. Supposing that Paul, after all a decently educated man in his time, might have something to say and might, in his own language, be saying it carefully; supposing further that as an apostle he might know whereof he speaks; supposing further that the task of Christian scholarship is to study the biblical sources before and not after making a decision about their relevance—it might just happen that by reading what Paul says without knowing beforehand that he is thinking about poltergeists and fairy godmothers, we could learn something useful.

And so, carefully almost to the point of seeming to plod, so unassumingly that the reader barely notices how much originality of perception he is profiting from, Berkhof reconstructs, one stone at a time, the formerly missing wing in the edifice of Paul's thought until we recognize, astonished, that it is habitable and weathertight. Few realms of thought are so apt to serve as demonstrations of the possibility, even—especially!—for modern man, of learning to grasp the inner logic and coherence of a thought world other than one's own.

Thanks to the labors of a generation of biblical theologians, what Professor Berkhof says in this booklet is not as new today as when the Dutch original appeared in

1953. Yet while a renewed awareness of the significance of the "Powers" is fast becoming common property among the theological technicians, no English publication has yet undertaken to share the new discovery more broadly with ordinary thinking Christians. Herald Press is warmly to be commended for making accessible this most helpful exposition.

For ten years Principal of the Theological Seminary of the Netherlands Reformed Church in Driebergen, Dr. Berkhof in 1960 became Professor of Dogmatic and Biblical Theology in the University of Leiden. A standard text in Church History (1942), *The Church and Caesar* (1946), a study of church-state relations in the age of Constantine, and *Christ the Meaning of History* (1958) are perhaps his most significant publications.

He was thrice elected a member of the Central Committee of the World Council of Churches (1954-1975). Since 1974 he is chairman of the Council of Churches in the Netherlands. *Christ and the Powers* was the first of his writings to be translated into English. It has since been followed by: *Christ the Meaning of History* (1958, ET 1966), *The Doctrine of the Holy Spirit* (ET 1964), *Well-Founded Hope* (1967, ET 1969). A systematic theology entitled *Christian Faith* (1973) is in process of translation.

John H. Yoder
Elkhart, Indiana

Author's Preface to the Second Edition

Now that a new edition of the English version is to appear, twenty-four years after the appearance of the Dutch original and fifteen years after the slightly expanded English translation, it may be proper to review something of the capricious history of this book.

It came into being out of a lecture which I presented about 1950 at a theological conference in Germany. Whoever knows anything of the situation of devastated and divided Germany in the early years of the cold war can hear an echo of that in the book. The listeners pressed for publication of the lecture. But I had to postpone the necessary reworking and expansion because of other duties, with the result that the text could not be published in Dutch until 1953. The publisher then offered it for translation to several German presses. There was no interest at all. I explain this as a result of the great changes that had taken place in West Germany in three years. Tension had significantly decreased and the welfare level was rising daily.

A short time later Miss Charlotte Von Kirschbaum, the secretary of Karl Barth, reported that she was enthusiastic about the book and had translated it into German, in order to have it published in the series *Theologische Studien,* which Barth edited. Not much later she had to write me her regrets that Barth had reasons not to let this text appear in his series. When in the summer of 1955 I was speaking with Barth about other things, he himself began lengthily to apologize for his refusal. He felt that I was "mythologizing" the Powers too much, and that he could not approve of such a publication at a time when his own theology was under the crossfire of Bultmann and his disciples.

Just a few years later, Dr. Yoder discovered the book. I owe him the first translation into English of any of my writings. I want to express here my gratitude for his initiative and his translation, and to both him and Herald Press for having had the nerve to bring to the American market a book by an unknown author. I am also happy that they are interested in a second edition.

When a few more years had passed I was completely convinced that the book was no longer of contemporary significance. But then I discovered that a translation into Japanese (from English) had been prepared, the work of Pastor Haruyoshi Fujimoto, who had studied in America. At that time (1969) Japan was in the midst of its great student uprisings which had awakened many questions about the direction of its culture. If I remember properly, a Professor Takenaka initiated the translation.

Now nine years later, in 1977, three things come to my attention. I have learned that the book is being translated from Dutch into Indonesian. The attention of a few theologians in Indonesia was drawn to it because of the battle which the churches in Indonesia need to wage against the supremecy of traditional mores (the so-called "adat"), and secondly because of the responsibility which they carry for the direction in which the rapid economic development of their country should go. The second report was that of Dr. Yoder who announced the possible English reprinting, since the book which at first sold rather slowly has in recent years been increasingly cited and sold.

The third observation was the publication of the last lectures of Karl Barth, dealing with Christian ethics, originally intended as bricks for the building of his Church Dogmatics IV, 4 *The Christian Life* (*Das Christliche Leben*, Zürich 1976). Within that text there appears a partial exposition of the Lord's Prayer. Under the second petition, "your kingdom come," Barth provides an extensive explanation concerning the "forces" which he calls "The Rebellious Powers." The way Barth treated this material came to me as a great surprise. Naturally this treatment goes immeasurably deeper than what I offer in this book, but it goes in the same direction. I feel sympathetic with this deepening treatment. I noticed with special interest that when Barth delivered these lectures (1961) he was clearly no longer bothered about the "mythologizing" which he had previously easily accused me of. On the contrary, he is now combating the modern spirit whose rational-scientific world view has no eye left for the power of the Powers. He testifies therefore that "one really even today can only speak of them with conscious mythologizing" (p. 367).

Why do I recount all this? Because it seems to me to show how much the capacity to recognize these thought patterns of the Apostle Paul has to do with the way in which a reader experiences and understands his own culture. There are many times and regions where these texts remain a sealed book. And then suddenly conditions can arise which make it visible that these words have a power to unveil and liberate.

Now that the book is coming out again in English, I had to consider to what extent changes should be made in a second edition. There would be much to favor the decision that after a quarter of a century the entire book should be rewritten. The world situation is very different; theological methods also. I would no longer be able to paint with such broad strokes as I then did. In both sociological and hermeneutic respects things would have to be more nuanced and refined in formulation. Likewise the opposition between church and world is much more complicated than I described it here. I would have to be much more precise about the Powers within the church. The concept of "Christianization" in chapter 6, which already then I limited and modified considerably, probably cannot be used at all anymore. I would also need to say more about ideologies. The great danger is just beginning to become clear that their function to conserve and to inspire human relations may be underestimated. And there would be more things to name.

Nonetheless, I have left the text unchanged. Subjectively, I have left it because it is extremely difficult for a writer to rewrite his own work. Objectively, because the spiritual and practical difference would be too little to justify the effort of rewriting. For the "message" of the book is still my own. It has continued to nourish my thinking in the following years. He who would read how these thoughts were inserted later in a wider context may read my *Christ the Meaning of History* (SCM, London, and John Knox, Richmond, Virginia, 1966). For me this book, just as I wrote it in 1952 and as it is now reprinted, still keeps something of the freshness of the "joy of discovery." I hope that something of that feeling can be true for those who read it for the first time.

In one footnote (19) I named some literature which had appeared on the subject between 1953 and the translation. This one section I have brought up-to-date. I have made no other changes. Whatever new readers find in the book, I hope it will help them to understand better the great Apostle Paul and to experience that Holy Scriptures has a word for every time.

Hendrik Berkhof
Oegstgeest, Netherlands

1

The Powers as a Challenge to Christian Thought

Introduction

The Apostle Paul repeatedly alludes to cosmic powers which play a definite role in relation to his faith in Christ. For the present we must let this vague phrase suffice to describe the realities we are about to study. Paul calls them "Powers" *(exousiae)*, in addition to various other names. To grasp what he means we must survey the texts in which Paul makes these allusions. We cite them here in the sequence in which we find them in our New Testament.[1]

> For I am sure that neither death nor life, nor angels nor principalities, nor present nor future, nor powers, nor height nor depth, nor any other creature, will be able to separate us from the love of God, which is in Christ Jesus, our Lord.—Romans 8:38 f.

None of the rulers of this age understood this [the hidden

wisdom of God]; for if they had, they would not have crucified the Lord of glory.—1 Corinthians 2:8.

Then comes the end, when He delivers the kingdom to God the Father, when He will have dethroned every rule, every power and dominion. For He must reign as king, until He has put all His enemies under His feet. The last enemy to be dethroned is death.—1 Corinthians 15:24-26.

. . . by raising Him from the dead and making Him sit at His right hand in the heavenly places, above every rule and power and might and dominion and every name that is named not only in this, but also in the coming age.—Ephesians 1:20 f.

. . . your trespasses and sins, in which you once walked, according to the course of this world, according to the prince of the power of the air, the spirit which is now at work in the children of disobedience.—Ephesians 2:1 f.

. . . that through the church the manifold wisdom of God shall be known to the principalities and powers in heavenly places.—Ephesians 3:10.

For we do not have to wrestle against flesh and blood, but against principalities and powers, against the world rulers of this darkness, against the evil spirits in heavenly places.—Ephesians 6:12.

For in Him are all things created, which are in heaven and on earth, the visible and the invisible, whether thrones, dominions, principalities, powers; all things are created through Him and for Him.—Colossians 1:16.

He disarmed the principalities and powers and made a public example of them, triumphing over them thereby.—Colossians 2:15

As we read these texts, the question arises at once whether the various terms Paul uses ("principalities, powers, thrones, dominions") indicate various sorts of

Powers, or various functions, or various names for more or less inclusive classifications. If it be the case that their meanings are distinct, this is never made clear, and is therefore not essential for an understanding of Paul's message. The fact that we find now one word, now two, three, or four, points in the same direction. We rather have the impression that Paul means to suggest broadly, by the variety of expressions, the number and diversity of the Powers.

The Renewed Significance of the Powers

In the last century little attention was devoted to this part of Paul's faith and thought. Either one read therein the confirmation of a conventional orthodox doctrine about angels and devils, or else they were seen as vestiges of antiquated mythology in Paul's thought, with which more enlightened ages need waste no time. The boundless quest for knowledge which characterized the nineteenth century did deal with these matters, but only incidentally and without noticeable effect. Just as in certain times certain aspects of the Holy Scriptures speak especially to a given generation, so also certain parts remain completely sealed. This was the case for Paul's doctrine of the Powers.[2]

In our century there has come a change, which has first of all been reflected in German theology. The German people have been especially prepared, both by character and by most recent history, for a new understanding of the "Powers." After World War I and especially after the rise of Nazism some theologians began reading these texts with new eyes. They discovered that instead of being antiquated, these passages found a strong resonance in the atmosphere of their own times.[3]

The Background in Comparative Religion

To attain to a clearer grasp of what Paul is getting at when he speaks of "principalities," "powers," "thrones," etc., . . . we need to investigate whether these words and concepts were used by his contemporaries or in other religious traditions with which he was acquainted. Research in this direction in recent decades has indicated that Paul's thought was not isolated from his intellectual and religious environment. Not that we find useful parallels in contemporary Greek philosophy, or—even less—in the religious thought of the Near East as a whole: but we do find a very distinct relatedness to certain lines of thought in the Jewish apocalyptic writings of Paul's time and the immediately preceding years. These writings, devoted to the exposition of heavenly mysteries, conceive of the "powers," "thrones," and the like as classes of angels located on higher or lower levels in the heavens. For that matter, all Jewish thought of the period was deeply interested in angels and their influences on terrestrial events. Also in the writings of the rabbis we often read about angels, thought of as holding authority over the forces of nature (stars, snow, hail). God rules the world, it was thought, not immediately, but through the services of countless angels. Bible readers will remember that . . . the apocalyptic Book of Daniel speaks of angels who serve as "princes" over the kingdoms of this world. Daniel 10:13, 20. All of this fits into a larger pattern when we think that the contemporary Near-Eastern nature religions believed in a hierarchy of intermediate beings, usually called "demons," between the divinity and this world. Yet again we must be careful not to make too broad the background of Paul's doctrine of the Powers. His terminology points us

most clearly to the above-named Jewish apocalyptic writings.[4]

We may therefore conclude that Paul's "Powers" terminology is not of his own invention. We cannot say that he borrowed it directly from Jewish apocalyptic, for that much we do not know. But at least it is definite that these terms were not new to the religious vocabulary of Paul's readers. We may in fact definitely assume that details in this terminology, which sound obtuse and even meaningless, were then clear and significant. This is true especially of the diversity of names which Paul gives to the Powers. Though we cannot discover in Paul's usage a real distinctness, such names are "technical" designations—for example, in the Book of *Enoch*—for various categories of angels. This shows that Paul borrowed the terms rather than creating them.

Thus the problem arises, whether or to what degree he gave to them a content differing from what they currently meant. Only in a later section can this question be answered, but in order to facilitate the investigation let us summarize what was essential to the view of the Powers found in the apocalyptic and rabbinic writings. Two things were always true of the Powers: (1) they are personal, spiritual beings and (2) they influence events on earth, especially events within nature. Armed with this knowledge we shall now investigate what Paul might have done with the same word. In so doing let us not take for granted that the above characteristic meanings hold true for his usage as well. This has usually been assumed, but it is scientifically improper. We must read from the words of Paul himself what the Powers meant to him; only then may we say whether and to what extent he shared current conceptions.

2
Paul's Conception of the Powers

We begin with the familiar text from Romans 8.

> For I am sure that neither death nor life, nor angels nor principalities, nor present nor future, nor powers, nor height nor depth, nor any other creature, will be able to separate us from the love of God, which is in Christ Jesus, our Lord.—Verse 38 f.

If we have begun to think of the Powers as angels or classes of angels, this text is somewhat embarrassing. The angelic names stand here side-by-side with other nouns which certainly do not designate personal spiritual beings. Even the sequence is most remarkable: death - life - angels - principalities - present - future - powers - height - depth; then all the list is summed up under the heading "creatures." Obviously Paul means to name a number of realities, which are a part of our earthly existence, and whose role is one of domination. This is still more evident in another text which also includes this kind of list, namely, 1 Corinthians 3:22:

> Whether Paul, Apollos, or Cephas; whether world, life, or death, whether present or future, all is yours.

Here the names of the angelic powers are missing, but here as well Paul intends to group the names of experienced realities which dominated the lives of the Corinthians. It is clear that these entities are not all thought of as persons, much less as angels. The fact that Paul could weave the names of the angelic powers into such a list of abstractions would indicate that his emphasis lies not on their personal-spiritual nature, but rather on the second characteristic named above, on the fact that these Powers condition earthly life.

Now we turn to 1 Corinthians 2:8:

> None of the rulers of this age understood this [hidden wisdom of God]; for if they had, they would not have crucified the Lord of glory.

It seems evident, and is almost always said by commentators, that "the rulers of this age" in this verse are not men, but superearthly realities identical with the "Powers" of which Paul speaks elsewhere. Here—in contrast to Romans 8:38 f.—they have a definitely personal aspect; they crucified the Lord of glory. Yet at the same time Paul's accent still seems to fall on the relation between the Powers and human history. Jesus was crucified by the high priests and the scribes, together with Herod and Pilate—in other words, by Jewish piety and law allied to the Roman state. In and behind these visible authorities, Paul sees invisible higher Powers working.[5]

The relationship between Christ's crucifixion and the Powers is treated more fully in Colossians 2, which is perhaps the most helpful in our understanding of their function, especially the verses 8, 14 ff., and 20 ff.:

> See to it that no one makes a prey of you by philosophy and empty deceit, according to human traditions, according to the *stoicheia* and not according to Christ. . . . He disarmed the principalities and powers and made a public example of them, triumphing over them thereby. . . . Therefore let no one pass judgment on you in questions of food and drink or with regard to a festival or a new moon or a sabbath, things which are only a shadow of what is to come, while the substance belongs to Christ. If then with Christ you have died to the **stoicheia**, why do you let regulations be laid on you, as if you still belonged to the world: "do not handle, do not taste, do not touch"? These are all things which perish as they are used, just as do human precepts and doctrines.

In quoting we left the word *stoicheia* untranslated. The context makes clear that Paul always uses it in connection with the "principalities and powers," so that this is either another name for such beings or a collective term for the earthly beings within which the Powers work. Therefore we must first attempt to grasp the word's meaning.[6]

For the present let us translate broadly—"world powers." The Powers rule over human life outside of Christ. They are manifested in human traditions (verse 8), in public opinion which threatens to entice the Christians in Colossae away from Christ. They are manifested in the cautious and timorous observance of requirements about abstinence from food and drink, or of feast days. Verses 16, 20 ff. All of this may be summed up as "prescriptions and doctrines of men." The "world powers" under which mankind languishes, to which the Colossians risk falling subject once again, are definite religious and ethical rules, the solid structures within which the pagan and the Jewish socieities of the day lived and moved. In verse 14 these structures are spoken of as the way in which the principalities and powers rule over men; or rather the powers *are* the structures. The main point is that by His cross Christ has unmasked and disarmed the quasi-divine authority of these structures.

We shall return to this, the main point of the text. Here we are asking what Paul thinks about the nature of the Powers and their connections with the world and human events. Therefore let us turn to Galatians 4:1-11, the other relevant text, where Paul speaks of the *stoicheia*, though without express reference to the other principalities and powers:

> As long as the heir is a child, he is no better than a slave, though he be the owner of all the estate; he is under guardianship and supervision until the time previously set by his father. Likewise we as well remained subjected to the world powers [*stoicheia*] as long as we were minor. But when the fullness of time had come, God sent forth His Son, born of woman, born under the law, to redeem those who were under the law, so that we should receive the right of sonship. And, since you are sons (God has sent the Spirit of His Son into our hearts, who cries, "Abba, Father!"), you are therefore no longer a slave, but a son, and if a son then also an heir. But when you did not know God, you served gods which are not really gods. Now that you have come to know God, or rather, to be known by God, how can you then turn again to the weak and beggarly world powers

[*stoicheia*] to whom you want to be subject once more? You observe days, months, seasons, and years. I fear that I have labored in vain over you.

Here again the world powers display both a pagan and a Jewish countenance. Again Paul addresses Christians, called out of paganism, who threaten to relapse into a Jewish-Christian pattern of thought, according to which they would be just as subject to the whole law as were the Jews. This means returning under the dominion of the world powers from which they had just been redeemed by Christ. Just as in Colossians, this dominion becomes manifest in men's enslavement to certain religious and ethical regulations. Once again, for the Gentiles this belonged in an astrological context, whereas for the Jews it meant literal obedience to Mosaic law. In both cases the result was the same; one seeks stability and structure for one's life in a scaffolding of laws, to which divine sanction is attributed (verse 8), a sanction irreconcilable with the claims of the new and greater Lord, Jesus Christ.

The texts thus far discussed permit a tentative summing up. Paul observes that life is ruled by a series of Powers. He speaks of time (present and future), of space (depth and height), of life and death, of politics and philosophy, of public opinion and Jewish law, of pious tradition and the fateful course of the stars. Apart from Christ man is at the mercy of these Powers. They encompass, carry, and guide his life. The demands of the present, fear for the future, state and society, life and death, tradition and morality—they are all our "guardians and trustees," the forces which hold together the world and the life of men and preserve them from chaos. We think of the desire expressed by Goethe's Faust:

> . . . that I may detect the utmost force, which binds the world and guides its course, its germ, productive powers explore. . . .—I, line 382.

The last phrase borrows from the language of alchemy, especially from Paracelsus, for whom the world "elements" had a similar meaning to what it bore for Paul's readers. It is the framework of creation, the canvas which invisibly supports the tableau of the life of men and society.

When we think back to the backgrounds in comparative religion, it is obvious that for Paul the Powers are something quite different from what Jewish apocalyptic circles had in mind. The influence of the angelic powers on earth, which for the apocalypticists was but one aspect of their nature, is all that Paul is interested in. While the apocalypses located this influence mainly in natural events (or perhaps in the state), Paul sees it as broad and as deep as life itself, and as especially connected with human affairs. Their angelic nature is—to say the least—not emphasized. Romans 8 and the study of the *stoicheia* do not lead us to think of personal beings (we shall discuss later the "angels" in Romans 8:38). The language of 1 Corinthians 2:8 is more personal, but even there we do not know whether to think of real beings or of figurative personification, a question we shall pursue later on. But the raising of this question is itself meaningful enough; it shows that in comparison to the apocalypticists a certain "demythologizing" has taken place in Paul's thought. In short, the apocalypses think primarily of the principalities and powers as heavenly angels; Paul sees them as structures of earthly existence.

This new burden of meaning is, so far as we can see, Paul's own creation. It arises from his vision of this world in the light of the reality of Christ. By the light of the liberation he discovers myriad forms of bondage. To give expression to the weight of such bondage he uses the current names for superterrestrial powers. The merit of the investigation of contemporary religious usage was that it acquainted us with this usage; yet this was also its weakness, since a similarity of terms and superficial parallels in meaning hid the deeper difference and thus led scholars to overlook Paul's originality.[7]

Powers and Angels

Thus far we have seen that Paul designates the Powers with the names of categories of angels, thought to have an influence on the course of events. The word *stoicheia* seems likewise to refer to angels, but in a more general and less personal tone. The personal aspect of the word "Powers" is likewise unaccented, while their influence upon events receives full emphasis (and furthermore a changed emphasis) compared to the usage of his time.

One can even doubt whether Paul conceived of the Powers as personal beings. In any case this aspect is so secondary that it makes little difference whether he did or not. He may be using personifications. He can also frequently write about sin and death as if they were persons. It is possible that he paints them with such personal traits because he sees them as tools of a personal Satan. But even should we be convinced that this "personal" way of speaking should be taken in full seriousness, it is still obvious that the pagan religious context, within which the personal character of these beings was most meaningful, is absent for him.

Separately from this we must now ask: Did Paul conceive of these "powers" as *angels*? This need not be identified with the question about their personal character; still it is generally assumed without discussion, on the grounds of other religious parallels. But for someone who has observed the great difference between the meaning of "Powers" for Paul and, for example, for *Enoch*, these parallels constitute no proof at all. It is rather remarkable that in the older theology (and in fact in theology up to our day) the Powers are understood as beings whose description belongs under the heading of "angels." At this one point traditional theology is in startling agreement with research in comparative religion. The equation "Powers=Angels" was probably drawn from Romans 8:38, where they are named together.

Yet theology in its expositions concerning angels has drawn hardly at all upon Paul's statements about the Powers. This seems strange at first, but was unavoidable. For what would we have to think of the "Powers" if we also thought of them as angels? Are they then good angels? Most have answered in the affirmative. But then what shall we do with the texts which speak of victory over, or combat with the Powers? How shall we understand that "all rule and all authority and power must be dethroned" as enemies? 1 Corinthians 15:24. If, on the other hand, we were to think of the fallen angels, how should we then explain the positive statements, which throw light upon their relation to creation, preservation, and reconciliation? More broadly, how could we connect "angels," as Paul does the Powers, to "present and future, life and death," "touch not, taste not?" There are too many difficulties to permit a careful theologian to think of taking seriously all that Paul says as describing the nature and function of angels.[8]

The conclusion is obvious; we must set aside the

thought that Paul's "Powers" are angels. Whether they be conceived as persons or as impersonal structures of life and society, they form a category of their own. The only fact which might point us to angels is the fact that in Romans 8:38 "powers" and "angels" are named in one breath. Yet we remember that the word *angelos* means more generally "messenger." It points not to a category of beings but to a function. Even when the word has a religious significance, it usually points to a being coming to men in God's name with a mediating function. Thus Paul in Romans 8:38 can call the Powers "God's messengers," since this describes very well the function he ascribes to them. (Cf. Colossians 1:16.) It is thus by no means the case that he is thinking of angels in the ordinary sense of the word; this is further contradicted by what he goes on to say about them.[9]

Thus far we have just begun our reconnoitering. Now the task is, by means of the insights thus far accumulated, to examine more closely all Paul's statements on the subject. This calls for a certain subdividing of the problem. He speaks of the Powers in connection with creation, with the Fall, with preservation, reconciliation, consummation, and the church. We shall examine each of these aspects in order.

3
The Powers and the Fallen Creation

Paul actually speaks of a connection between the Powers and creation in only one text, but this is a very weighty and a very clear one:

> He is the image of the invisible God, the firstborn of the whole creation; for in Him are all things created, which are in heaven and on earth, the visible and the invisible, whether thrones, dominions, principalities, powers; all things are created through Him and for Him. He is before all things and in Him all things have their being.—Colossians 1:15-17.

Usually the expositors of these words have laid all the accent on their negative aspect. They see (rightly) Paul's polemic against certain ideas, then influential in the churches of Asia Minor, according to which the world was ruled by a series of spiritual beings. Paul's use of four names is a definite allusion to the angelic hierarchy, which was imagined in terms which were apparently related to those in *Enoch.* Paul hereby says: Jesus Christ, not these powers, rules the world! The Powers are nothing but impotent servants, instruments of His dominion! Yet we should see beyond this negative, polemic intent, which is but the obverse of a positive insight. Paul does not reject the Powers as pagan imaginings. Had his intent been purely polemic, this would have been the most effective. But though he does downgrade them because of Christ, he at the same time recognizes their positive significance, which is the point we are interested in here.

Paul confesses Jesus Christ, crucified and risen, as the ground and the goal of the universe. He is the key and the secret of all creation. This creation comprises a visible and an invisible, or an earthly and a heavenly part. We might better say: Creation has a visible foreground, which is bound together with and dependent on an invisible background. This latter comprises the Powers. These as well were created through and unto Christ; that is, God's love, the same which came to us in Christ, is also the ground and the goal of the Powers. They *are* subservient to this love; they did not first need to be made subservient. From their very creation, by their very nature, they were "made to measure" to serve as instruments of this love.

We read, "All things have their being in Him." The Greek verb is *synhesteken*, related to our word "system." Christ—and not the Powers themselves—is the system of creation. In subjection to Him, who is "head" and "beginning" (verse 18), everything is in its proper, divinely intended place. Then the Powers serve as the invisible weight-bearing substratum of the world, as the underpinnings of creation. By no means does Paul think of the Powers as evil in themselves. They are the linkage between God's love and visible human experience. They are to hold life together, preserving it within God's love, serving as aids to bind men fast in His fellowship; intermediaries, not as barriers but as bonds between God and man. As aids and signposts toward the service of God, they form the framework within which such service must needs be carried out.

It strikes us as strange that Paul can speak thus positively of what he elsewhere calls "poor and weak powers of this world" or "precepts and doctrines of men." Yet it is not so strange. Divers human traditions, the course of earthly life as conditioned by the heavenly bodies, morality, fixed religious and ethical rules, the administration of justice and the ordering of the state—all these can be tyrants over our life, but *in themselves* they are not. These fixed points are not the devil's invention; they are the dikes with which God encircles His good creation, to keep it in His fellowship and protect it from chaos. This is true of time ("life and death, present and future"), and of space ("height and depth"), within which our existence is held fast. They correspond approximately to what theologians would call the "Orders." No demonic revolt of the Orders can make us forget that evil can never create anything; thus the Orders as such cannot be evil, but must rather have a positive value in God's world plan. They can preserve us in Christ's love. It is precisely when they do this that they fulfill their own destiny. Therefore the believer's combat is never to strive *against* the Orders, but rather to battle for God's intention for them, and against their corruption.

The Powers and the Fall

Paul speaks, once, of the Powers as related to the creative will of God. But we do not know them in this divinely intended role. We know them only as bound up with the enigmatic fact of sin, whereby not only men have turned away from God, but the invisible side of the cosmos functions in diametric opposition to its divinely fixed purpose. When Paul writes that nothing can separate us from the love of Christ, not even the Powers, he presupposes that the nature of the Powers would be to do just that, to separate us from love. The Powers are no longer instruments, linkages between God's love, as revealed in Christ, and the visible world of creation. In fact, they have become gods (Galatians 4:8), behaving as though they were the ultimate ground of being, and demanding from men an appropriate worship. This is the demonic reversal which has taken place on the invisible side of creation. No longer do the Powers bind man and God together; they separate them. They stand as a roadblock between the Creator and His creation.

The Powers continue to fulfill one half of their function. They still undergird human life and society and preserve them from chaos. But by holding the world together, they hold it away from God, not close to Him. They are "the rulers of this age" (1 Corinthians 2:6). In their desire to rule they are in enmity toward the Lord of glory, who can suffer them only as instruments, not as lords. Paul touches on this in a remarkable way in Ephesians 2:1, saying that Gentile believers had previously walked "according to the course of the world, according to the prince of the power of the air." The "prince" is evidently Satan. He rules the course of this world and does so with the help of "the power" (which, however, is singular here) "of the air," that is, which resides in the air, thence exerting its force on earth. According to Ephesians 6:12 the Powers reside "in the heavenly regions." Both expressions mean the same thing. "Heavenly places" clearly refers not to heaven as the place of God's special presence, but to the atmosphere around the earth. This is parallel to Colossians 1:16, where the Powers are thought of as being in heaven.

What does Paul mean to say by means of this peculiar spatial reference and especially with the word "air"? The cosmology of the time distinguished several "heavens": heaven as God's residence, the heaven of the stars, and (between the earth and the moon) the air-heaven. The last of these belongs next to the earth as the invisible, higher sphere of influence from within which the earth is ordered. The "air" is the sphere which binds together the divine and the human worlds. Yet the Powers, which have their domicile here, are subject to a ruler, who permits them to determine "the course of this world" in such a way that men walk "in trespasses and sins," as "children of disobedience." Subject to "the power of the air," we are "without hope and without God in the world" (verse 12). This renders still more evident what liberation is wrought by the message that Christ has broken through this sphere, "descended to the lower, earthly regions" (Ephesians 4:9), so that since then the believer is assured that neither powers nor dominions can separate us from God's love in Christ.

We have been speaking of ancient cosmology, in connection with the word "air." Here, however, as well as with many other biblical expressions usually thought to be borrowed from this cosmology, the question arises whether the world view we need to deal with is not the more "natural" one, given to us as part of our being human, which is pre-intellectual, experienced and understood by every man. For man, erect of carriage, with his spiritual capacities located in the uppermost part of the body, the best is naturally "above" and evil "below." God and heaven belong together. The Powers which rule our life, though not divine, exercise their dominion from above. We ourselves say, even more literally, that "something is in the air."

When Hitler took the helm in Germany in 1933, the Powers of *Volk*, race, and state took a new grip on men. Thousands were grateful, after the confusion of the preceding years, to find their lives again protected from chaos, order and security restored. No one could withhold himself, without utmost effort, from the grasp these Powers had on men's inner and outer life. While studying in Berlin (1937) I myself experienced almost literally how such Powers may be "in the air." At the same time one had to see how they intruded as a barrier between God's Word and men. They acted as if they were ultimate values, calling for loyalty as if they were the gods of the cosmos.

I allude to this example solely because it makes so strikingly clear the sense of Paul's expressions (not only his meaning but also his actual terms). Nor should it be difficult for us to perceive today in every realm of life these Powers which unify men, yet separate them from God. The state, politics, class, social struggle, national interest, public opinion, accepted morality, the ideas of decency, humanity, democracy—these give unity and direction to thousands of lives. Yet precisely by giving unity and direction they separate these many lives from the true God; they let us believe that we have found the meaning of existence, whereas they really estrange us from true meaning.

The Powers and Conservation

We already noted that even in the fallen world the Powers retain one side of their divinely established function. They are still the framework of creation, preserving it from disintegration. They are the dike which prevents the chaotic deluge from submerging the world. This is of extreme importance, as Paul very well understands. He expresses this insight in Galatians 4:1-11, the passage we already discussed in relation to the *stoicheia.* There he reminds his readers that they formerly had lived under the world powers, before they learned to know the living God in Jesus Christ. This was their time of "minority" (verse 3). When man is redeemed by Christ, he is freed from slavery to the Powers and becomes a child of God, dependent solely and wholly on Him and obedient to Him. Verse 4. This does not involve an absolute condemnation of the earlier subservience to the Powers. Such subservience was inevitable, yea, a work of God's goodness. Since man outside of Christ is a "minor," unable to find his way, helpless and without direction, his life would be abandoned to dissolution if the Powers were not there, to whom men instinctively entrust themselves; for God has made for each other the visible and the invisible sides of the cosmos, that is, men and the Powers. Man outside Christ stood, thanks to God's preserving care, "under guardians and trustees."

The Powers take us in trust, hold our lives within a sure enclosure, saving them for the time when preservation will be overtaken and included in the more far-reaching work of redemption. Thus in the world alienated from God the Powers have a very positive function. They keep men alive. We must hasten to say that such a "life" is not fully worthy of the name; it is life "improperly so-called," a life under guardians, in slavery, within which man falls short of his destined end. Contrasted with the life of divine sonship it can scarcely bear the name "life." Yet in contrast to the chaos, to which our enmity toward God has condemned to us, life under the Powers is tolerable, even good.[10]

This understanding is especially illuminating when we think of the religio-social structures by which the world outside Christ has been and is carried along. Certain powers give cohesion to life, fixing the path for the individual as well as for society. We may think of the place of the clan or tribe among primitive peoples, or of the respect for ancestors and the family which for centuries gave form and content to Chinese life. We may point to Shintoism in Japan, to the Hindu social order in India, to the astrological unity of ancient Babel, to the deep significance of the *polis* or city-state for the Greeks, or to the Roman state. It is no less evident that the modern world as well is ruled by *stoicheia.* However pointedly the Bible teaches us to see this as slavery, we should not forget that it is still a part of God's preserving mercy, holding life in line where men do not know Christ's liberation. The manifold moral traditions and codes of which moral life is full are examples. Clearly, these as well reveal their tyrannical character, whether they will or no, in the encounter with Christ. In a world where Christ is preached there is no longer room for them in the positive function they filled in the pre- and extra-Christian world. When unmasked they lose their totalitarian, conserving hold on life, or else they become anti-Christian powers, as we have seen the powers of race, class, state, and *Volk* doing in Nazism and communism. We shall give further attention to the place of the Powers in the world after Christ's coming.

these are anti-Christian? others reveal "their tyrannical ~~not~~ character ... in the encounter with Christ" are they not anti-christian, or simply irrelevant

Would Berkhof differ from Dooyeweerd in that D. would see Powers as among things to be redeemed? or are they simply put back into their proper + more limited place?

4

The Powers in Redemption

When Jesus was crucified and rose from the dead, and since then wherever this saving event is proclaimed, the domination of the world powers is at an end. This certainly is the center of everything Paul says about the Powers. It is in the light of this event that the Powers and their enmity toward God are made manifest and by the same token that an end is put to their working. The most significant text where Paul expresses this conviction is the section of Colossians 2 to which we have often referred:

> And you, though you were dead through your trespasses and uncircumcision according to the flesh, He has made alive together with Him, acquitting us of all our trespasses by canceling the writ which was established against us and threatened us with its demands; this He eliminated by nailing it to the cross. He disarmed the principalities and powers and made a public example of them, triumphing over them thereby.—Verses 13-15.

Paul is discussing reconciliation by the cross of Christ. He speaks repeatedly of this theme, but here the emphasis is different. Atonement here is not only (as elsewhere) a redemption of the sinner from guilt, but especially liberation from slavery to the powers of fate. This bondage does not replace our guilt; it is rather a consequence of guilt. Thus he can speak of the acquittal of all our trespasses; but the acquittal also makes an end to our bondage to the Powers. This latter point is what especially interests Paul in this connection.

We usually understand the "legal demands" of which he speaks as meaning the curse of the law in the sense of which we read in Romans or Galatians. But this term (Greek *dogmata*, AV "ordinances") is directly connected to the verb *dogmatizein* in verse 20, where it is translated "to impose regulations." The *dogmata* in question are: "Handle not, taste not, touch not"; in verse 22 they are called "human precepts and doctrines." Doubtless Paul is thinking, as in Galatians 4, of the Mosaic law, understood not as a manifestation of God's holy will, but as a power which unites the Jewish people socially and religiously, and simultaneously alienates them from God. Likewise this law, just as its Gentile equivalent, is "empty deceit, according to human tradition, according to the world spirits, and not according to Christ" (verse 8). In a closely related text, Ephesians 2, the "law of commandments and ordinances" (verse 15) is equated with Jewish law, which like a wall divided the Jews from the Gentiles. Here the thought is the same. The choice of words shows how Paul can view Jewish law and pagan regulations as essentially alike and both as overcome through Christ's cross.

By the cross (which must always, here as elsewhere, be

seen as a unit with the resurrection) Christ abolished the slavery which, as a result of sin, lay over our existence as a menace and an accusation. On the cross He "disarmed" the Powers, "made a public example of them and thereby triumphed over them." Paul uses three different verbs to express more adequately what happened to the Powers at the cross.

He "made a public example of them." It is precisely in the crucifixion that the true nature of the Powers has come to light. Previously they were accepted as the most basic and ultimate realities, as the gods of the world. Never had it been perceived, nor could it have been perceived, that this belief was founded on deception. Now that the true God appears on earth in Christ, it becomes apparent that the Powers are inimical to Him, acting not as His instruments but as His adversaries. The scribes, representatives of the Jewish law, far from receiving gratefully Him who came in the name of the God of the law, crucified Him in the name of the law. The priests, servants of His temple, crucified Him in the name of the temple. The Pharisees, personifying piety, crucified Him in the name of piety. Pilate, representing Roman justice and law, shows what these are worth when called upon to do justice to the Truth Himself. Obviously, "none of the rulers of this age," who let themselves be worshiped as divinities, understood God's wisdom, "for had they known, they would not have crucified the Lord of glory" (1 Corinthians 2:8). Now they are unmasked as false gods by their encounter with very God; they are made a public spectacle.

Thus Christ has "triumphed over them." The unmasking is actually already their defeat. Yet this is only visible to men when they know that God Himself had appeared on earth in Christ. Therefore we must think of the resurrection as well as of the cross. The resurrection manifests what was already accomplished at the cross: that in Christ God has challenged the Powers, has penetrated into their territory, and has displayed that He is stronger than they.

The concrete evidence of this triumph is that at the cross Christ has "disarmed" the Powers. The weapon from which they heretofore derived their strength is struck out of their hands. This weapon was the power of illusion, their ability to convince men that they were the divine regents of the world, ultimate certainty and ultimate direction, ultimate happiness and the ultimate duty for small, dependent humanity. Since Christ, we know that this is illusion. We are called to a higher destiny; we have higher orders to follow and we stand under a greater Protector. No Powers can separate us from God's love in Christ. Unmasked, revealed in their true nature, they have lost their mighty grip on men. The cross has disarmed them; wherever it is preached, the unmasking and the disarming of the Powers takes place.

In what way and to what extent this happens we shall discuss further. For him who sees and believes this, it means an immense liberation, to which Paul points clearly: "If you have died with Christ to the world powers, why do you let commands be laid upon you, as if you were still in the world: 'Handle not, taste not, touch not'?"

The Powers and Consummation

That Christ has unmasked and disarmed the Powers does not mean that with one blow their ungodly working has been put to a stop. In principle the victory is certain;

yet the battle continues until the triumph will have become effective on all fronts and visible to all. In what sense, and to what degree, the victory is already effective, a later chapter will investigate. Here our interest is in observing that, because of what happened in the cross and resurrection, the godless dominion of the Powers shall one day come to an end, completely and definitively. This is Paul's theme in 1 Corinthians 15. One day Christ shall turn over His kingship to God the Father, "when He shall have dethroned every rule and every authority and power" (verse 24); and just a little later, "the enemy to be dethroned is death" (verse 28).

It is not as feasible as it might at first seem to penetrate fully the purport of these words. Some translations (for example, the RSV) speak not of "dethroning" but of "destroying," which is quite different. In one case the Powers no longer exist at the end; in the other they do. The Greek word used by Paul can have either meaning. "Destroy" seems at first a little more likely; let us begin with it.

Shall we suppose that in the kingdom life would no longer be held together by definite Powers and Orders? It is conceivable that this could be Paul's meaning. The unmediated contemplation of God's presence and fellowship could make all more external forms of cohesion and of community superficial. Such an interpretation would be perfectly fitting for death.

Yet there are good reasons to doubt this. Earlier we noted that the Powers form the invisible aspect of God's good creation. In themselves they are not evil. The thought that they should be annihilated in the ultimate consummation, so that the whole undergirding of creation would fall away, would have called for a clearer statement, had Paul really sought to make this point; he probably did not intend such a meaning. In Colossians 1, after saying that the Powers were created in Christ and have in Him their Head, he moves directly from creation to reconciliation and to new creation and concludes:

> For all the fullness was pleased to dwell in Him, and through Him, having made peace by the blood of His cross, to reconcile with Himself all things, whether on earth or in heaven.—Verse 19.

The words, "or in heaven," point back to verse 16, where the Powers are alluded to as the higher, invisible aspect of created reality. God reconciles the Powers—and not only men—with Himself through Christ's death. This thought is strange to us; we usually think of reconciliation as an act relating only to persons. Here Paul uses it in a broader sense, as meaning a restoration of proper relationships. In this sense the Powers as well are object of God's plan of redemption. By virtue of this purpose they will no longer lie between man and God as a barrier, but can and shall return to their original function, as instruments of God's fellowship with His creation. The same truth can be glimpsed in Ephesians 1:10, where God's saving purpose is stated thus: "as a plan for the fullness of time, to bring together under one Head, even Christ, all that is in heaven or on earth." The Powers which now seek headship for themselves will be subjected to their true Head, Christ.

Such statements indicate strongly that Powers are present even in the consummation, that there also there shall be formed and ordered life, but in such a way that these forms and orders are nothing more than the undergirding of the perfected communion between God and His creation. Thus it can further be said that Christ is exalted above all powers and above "every name that is named, not only in this age but also in that which is to come" (verse 21). "Name" and "Power" here are interchangeable. Paul thus says in so many words that the Powers have their role also in the age to come.[11]

For this reason we must reject the translation "destroy" in 1 Corinthians 15:24, 26 and prefer "dethrone." The Greek verb *katargein* means literally "to make ineffective," "to disconnect." The Powers are put out of commission as enemies (verse 26), which means in the light of the other texts just studied that at the same stroke they are reinstated in their proper function within Christ's lordship. How this shall be, and what function the structures of our life shall have in the age to come, Paul does not say. He presumably felt that men of our endowments cannot grasp or imagine this.

If we have thus far understood Paul properly, a difficulty remains in connection with verse 26, "the last enemy to be dethroned is death." Does this mean that even death shall have a place in the restored creation? We observed in Romans 8:38 that Paul counts death as one of the Powers or at least as closely related to them. But this consequence forces us to look closer. Can it be that for Paul, who so emphatically and so frequently connects death with sin, dying at the same time has about it something natural? What would this natural aspect be? Would it be the fact that God's goodness may put an end to our earthly existence, the gift of finite time of which Barth speaks?[12]

Even if this question were to be answered affirmatively (for which the grounds are lacking), we would stand before a still more difficult one: What function could such a finitude of life possibly have in the age to come? There are still fewer grounds for answering this. What interests Paul in the context cited is solely that death as enemy, as curse and as judgment, as wages of sin, is utterly divested of its power. Though he knows that redeemed life also has its powers, its forms and framework, his whole interest is in saying that Christ (and the Father, 1 Corinthians 15:28) shall be radically and unambiguously Head and Lord, and that the enslaving and seductive effort of the world powers is broken for good.

The Limitation of the Powers

The Powers are already unmasked and disarmed, and shall imminently be dethroned. "Already" and "not yet" are the poles of the tension which dominates the entire New Testament proclamation. For faith this is no contradiction, any more than it was contradictory for us in the Netherlands during the "hunger winter" (1944-45) that the Nazis, defeated, were still oppressing us. It may be difficult to express to what extent one statement or the other is true, to find words to do justice to both. Yet much depends, for faith and for life, on a proper insight into tension. If we wish to speak faithfully of our attitude toward the Powers in this intermediate age, we cannot leave to one side this question, which is one of the basic problems, if not *the* basic problem of New Testament theology. Our title speaks of "limiting" the Powers. The term is an effort to combine the "already" and the "not yet." The Powers are still present; but wherever Christ is preached and believed in, a limit has been set to their working. This limit is the sign and the promise of their defeat.

Primarily this limitation is seen in the continued existence of the church of Christ. By her very presence she breaks through that unshaken stability of life under the Powers, which we know and marvel at in ancient civilizations. She is made up of men who see through the deception of the Powers, refusing to run after isms. Standing within the community of a people or a culture, their presence is an interrogation, the questioning of the legitimacy of the Powers. By her faith and life the church of Christ labels the dominion of the Powers as *un-self-evident.* She is the turnstile which shuts off all return to the unconscious taken-for-grantedness of the former cultures.

Yet before and apart from this the Powers are limited by the very presence of men who will no longer let themselves be enslaved, led astray, and intimidated, against whom the program of the Powers, that is, their effort to separate men from God, suffers shipwreck. Even outside the church there are some men against whom some Powers are ineffective, but that is no complete shipwreck. In such persons another Power is working more powerfully than those which rule other men; Power strives against Power. Where all Powers are seen to be subjected to Jesus Christ, who is made Head over all things for the church (Ephesians 1:22), something quite different has happened. It is then inevitable that the Powers should resort to oppression and persecution. But in this very act of desperation (which also distinguishes our age from that before Christ) their unmasking is repeated and confirmed. They can no longer exist without being forced to uncover their true nature and thereby to abandon their role as gods and saviors. Christ brings the Powers to a crisis, whose breadth and significance we shall study in a later chapter.

There is still another, still more important sense in which the Powers are limited. Since Christ, the Powers can no longer attain their goal. In spite of themselves they have been made subservient to Him in whom all is brought together under one Head. One thing they can attempt: they can seek to banish the memory of Christ and the signs of His lordship from men's awareness in order to renew their own unchallenged dominion with a "pseudo-Messianic counterrevolution." But this does not succeed. On the contrary, again at every turn, there remains of their effort only that which can find its place in God's plan. The New Testament is full of this confidence. The whole Book of Revelation testifies to it. Though we do not happen to possess express statements of Paul on the subject, we need not doubt that for him as well, all the work and the wrath is directed and transformed by God's greater might. The most beautiful testimony to this belief is the prayer of the first church, especially these words:

> For truly there gathered together in this city against thy holy servant Jesus, whom thou didst anoint, Herod and Pontius Pilate with the Gentiles and the peoples of Israel, to do whatever thy hand and thy plan had determined should happen.—Acts 4:27 f.

All the anti-Christian Powers can achieve nothing but what fits into the saving divine counsel. Even in their opposition they are God's collaborators. Their function as instruments of God, given them in creation, which shall be fully restored in the new creation, is already inescapable since the victory of Christ.

With this aspect of limitation another is closely connected; God makes an end to the Powers' dominion in that repeatedly He stops them in their tracks. It may be to shackle or to free them; in either case they follow the triumph-wagon of the conquering Christ as slaves. We see an expression of this in Jesus' dealing with the evil spirits. He did not set about expelling and systematically combating them. Precisely because they were limited by His victory, there was no need for this. But whenever they cross His path and seek to resist His work, He calls them inexorably to a halt. The spirits ask, "Have you come to torture us before the time" (Matthew 8:29)? But the time is fulfilled. The shadow of the great "Halt!" at the end of the times falls already today, repeatedly, upon His adversaries. But just as well where it does not ring out, the "halt!" which the Powers sought to oppose to Christ's advance fades away powerless as they are fitted into God's kingdom plan in spite of themselves.

5

The Church and the Powers

It is given to the church as a privilege—and therefore as a duty—to take toward the Powers, restrained as they are by God, yet still seductive and menacing, a definite stance. This stance is grounded in the fact that, by virtue of their fellowship with the Lord of all the Powers, believers have been enabled to see through their anti-Christian dimension. When Paul lists (1 Corinthians 12:8-10) the various gifts of the Spirit which are bestowed upon the church, he names among them the "discernment of spirits." In the church the distinction becomes clear between movings of spirits which are of and unto God and those which are of and unto the evil one. This involves especially the discerning of the Powers which hold the hearts and actions of men under their sway in specific times and places.

Paul makes clear that this is a special gift of the Spirit, which not everyone possesses, at least not in the same measure. The Spirit distributes the gifts in a special way to each person, as He wills. Verse 11. Kierkegaard possessed the gift in far greater measure than Martensen; Martin Niemöller, than *Reichsbischof* Müller. But really the word "more" is out of place here. I have chosen just these names precisely because they demonstrate that, seen from outside, this discernment of spirits is a very problematic matter. There is prophecy and there is false prophecy. But the rule of the Holy Spirit consists in this, that the church which lives in true fellowship with her Lord can distinguish between the shepherds and the hirelings. This rule is manifest when false prophecy withers away, while the true becomes fruitful in the church and in the world.

When the Powers are unmasked, they lose their dominion over men's souls and the jubilant exclamation arises, "Nothing can separate us from the love of God in Christ Jesus!" Yet this rejoicing is also broken, ambiguous. The believer is "still but a man." As a sinful man he senses in his own flesh the seduction and the threats of the Powers, and, still worse, he feels himself an unbeliever, going unwittingly the way of all men. Yet by the might of the indwelling Holy Spirit the strength of the Powers is limited, also, in the life of the individual believer. Somehow he escapes the temptations and the treats. Somehow his Christian liberty bursts through their servitude. In critical times this liberation can be so mightily manifested as to be externally tangible, as, for example, when a Christian church must live in the midst of a demonically nationalistic society, or in a communistic world poisoned by terror and espionage.

From this discernment there springs forth a basically different way of dealing with creaturely reality. The

Holy Spirit "shrinks" the Powers before the eye of faith. They may well have inflated themselves into omnipotent total value systems, but the believer sees them in their true proportions, as nothing more than one segment of creation, existing because of the Creator, and limited by other creatures. The Nazis spoke of "nationhood," where the confessing church said "the nation" or preferably "the nations." In our Christian circles we would rather say "the authorities" than "the state." This is not so much because the two terms are not quite logically equivalent, as because of a wholesome intuition, seeing in "state" an autonomous power, whereas with "authorities" we think of ordinary men in higher positions. Where the Spirit of Christ rules, Mammon shrivels down to "finances," conventional morality to a set of rules of thumb, subject to criticism and limited in scope and authority. Changing customs, slogans, and isms of the moment are seen as ideas which are merely "in the air," worth no more and no less than the older slogans they replaced. Where the victorious kingship of Christ is confessed, there prevails a consistent unbelief in the utility of military power, and national or international armament is at the most grudgingly accepted as a bitter duty of responsible citizenship. Anxiety before the fearsome future gives way to a simple carefulness, since we know that the future as well is in God's hands.

And so we could go on. . . . In faith life is seen and accepted in its smallness and modesty. All that God has created is good; nothing is to be rejected if it is received with thanksgiving. 1 Timothy 4:4. The believer does not flee the world, but he avoids deifying it. For him the world is "de-deified." In this sense there is a real place for a Christian avoidance of the world. The "weak" need to avoid certain realms of the world, because the Powers who reign there would draw them away from their fellowship with their Lord.

The strong can express this "avoidance of the world" in other ways, even by walking through the middle of its kingdoms, withstanding undaunted by their action and their very presence, like the young men in the fiery furnace. In so doing we must constantly remind ourselves: we do not belong to the nation, the state, the technique, the future, the money, but all this is ours, given us by God as means of living a worthy life before God and in fellowship with our neighbor.[13]

In all that we have said about the Christian's stance toward the Powers the element of withdrawal predominates. This may seem negative. Has he not also a more positive and aggressive responsibility? Ephesians 3:10 points in this direction, when Paul describes as the goal of his ministry "that through the church the manifold wisdom of God might now be made known to the principalities and powers in the heavenly places." What does he mean to say? The "heavenly places" are doubtless identical with the "air" of which 2:2 had spoken. But what wisdom should the church announce to the Powers, and how?

Paul's statement is made in connection with the truth that since Christ a new force has made its entry on the stage of salvation history: the church. She is something quite different from Israel as God's people. She is an undreamed-of synthesis of the two sorts of men who people the world, Jews and Gentiles. That Christ has brought both together into one body is the mystery, which for ages had remained hidden (verse 9) but has come to light, thanks to Paul's ministry. In this ministry is manifested "the unsearchable wealth of Christ" (verse 8) and the "manifold wisdom of God" (verse 10).

This is what the church announces to the Powers. The very existence of the church, in which Gentiles and Jews, who heretofore walked according to the *stoicheia* of the world, live together in Christ's fellowship, is itself a proclamation, a sign, a token to the Powers that their unbroken dominion has come to an end. Thus even this text says nothing of a positive or aggressive approach to the Powers. Such an approach is superfluous because the very presence of the church in a world ruled by the Powers is a superlatively positive and aggressive fact. We have already dealt with what this fact means to the Powers, for whom it is a sign of the end time, of their incipient encirclement and their imminent defeat.

This same fact is also freighted with meaning for the Christian. All resistance and every attack against the gods of this age will be unfruitful, unless the church herself *is* resistance and attack, unless she demonstrates in her life and fellowship how men can live freed from the Powers. We can only preach the manifold wisdom of God to Mammon if our life displays that we are joyfully freed from his clutches. To reject nationalism we must begin by no longer recognizing in our own bosoms any difference between peoples. We shall only resist social injustice and the disintegration of community if justice and mercy prevail in our own common life and social differences have lost their power to divide. Clairvoyant and warning words and deeds aimed at state or nation are meaningful only in so far as they spring from a church whose inner life is itself her proclamation of God's manifold wisdom to the "Powers in the air."

This is not to say that Paul is ignorant of a more direct

encounter between the faithful and the Powers. Ephesians 6:10-18 proves the contrary. The believer strives ultimately not against tangible men and objects ("flesh and blood," verse 12), but against the Powers they obey. This war with the Powers must be waged seriously. A man must arm himself for it. The arms named (truth, righteousness, the readiness of the gospel of peace, faith, salvation, and the Word of God) show that Paul is not contemplating an offensive against the Powers. Though surely the believer must assure his defense against them, he can do this only by standing, simply, by his faith. He is not called to do more than he can do by simply believing. His duty is not to bring the Powers to their knees. This is Jesus Christ's own task. He has taken care of this thus far and will continue to do so.

We are responsible for the defense, just because He takes care of the offense. Ours it is to hold the Powers, their seduction and their enslavement, at a distance, "to be able to stand against the wiles of the devil" (verse 11, cf. 13). The figurative allusion to weapons points to this defensive role. Girdle, breastplate, shoes, shield, helmet, and sword (*machaira*, the short sword) are all defensive arms. Lance, spear, bow, and arrow are not named. They are not needed; these are the weapons Christ Himself bears. Our weapon is to stay close by Him and thus to remain out of the reach of the drawing power of the Powers.

6
Crisis and Christianization of the Powers

All of this certainly does not mean that Christ's church stands as a solitary island amidst an unbroken sea of hostility. Just by being simply the church, she is the instrument whereby Christ brings to *crisis* the rule of the Powers even far outside her borders. The exalted Lord does not reveal His lordship only by founding the church. Outside her borders He is just as active, making manifest His victory. This victory is for Paul not only in the future; it is already effective in this dispensation. Thus we can go one step beyond speaking only of "limitation" (as in Chapter 4). Christ's incarnation and self-sacrifice on the cross already involve restoring the heavenly Powers to their proper position. Colossians 1:20. This is already now God's purpose,

> . . . in preparation for the fullness of time, to unite under one head, that is, Christ, everything in heaven and on earth.

The ineffable reality behind these words is best illustrated when we give attention to what happens when the mission breaks into a pre-Christian or extra-Christian culture. A complete disintegration of social life, which previously was ruled by certain Powers, takes place. Life is stirred up, desacralized, "de-deified," in that the new Lord makes His entry. As it is this Lord who enters, this is not evil, but for the good of all.

We know the tales and testimonies of men who were released by Christ from the bondage of the Powers that had driven them, now released to freedom and humanity. This peace with God in Christ then creates its own new patterns of life, within which the Powers take the modest and purely instrumental place which was meant for them.

We must not fail to recognize that the proclamation of Christ as Lord over the Powers can with time lead to directly opposite, fatal results. The enemies of the Christian mission have had a sharp nose for such things. What happens when the new Lord does not lay, or can no longer lay, His claims on men and on the Powers? We might think that the former life under the Powers as "guardians and trustees" should return, and the conditions be restored which were obtained before the preaching of the gospel.

But we know that this does not happen. It cannot. When Christ's rule has come on the scene, there is no "return." If the positive signs of His control are missing, the negative signs remain, ineradicably burned into men's souls. In spite of themselves men confess His kingship. The desacralizing of the world cannot be undone. The Powers once dethroned cannot return as if nothing had happened.

Who the cup to his lips has once set,
His soul now of innocence is bereft,
His flesh has been pierced by Heaven.
Though the water be turned to wine,
The dregs will yet poison his soul
With a thirst that can never be slaked
At a spring he might find here below.
Who once tasted the heavenly bread,
In the brute the Eternal did graft,
Has mortgaged his life at the price
Of a festering double death.[15]

We have come to what in our opinion is the key to our age's cultural crisis, in Asia as well as in Europe, in fact, in practically the whole world. Everywhere the preaching of Christ as Lord has brought an end to the stable reign of the Powers. The crisis of the Powers is still in effect where Christ can no longer (as in Europe) or not yet (Asia) lay hold on the life of peoples. The proclamation has gone out from Europe, but even more has its negative aspect, the dethroning of the Powers. Where the latter is not accompanied by the former, there exists a cultural crisis of the greatest seriousness. Life has lost its old unity without finding another.

What solution can there be to this crisis? One possibility is secularization. In such a life many Powers have a certain place, but no single one plays a total, unifying role: life goes on with no center. Thus may be characterized the life of today's "cultured world." The Powers of a humanistic ideal of personality, of a decent human existence, of public morality, of Mammon, Eros, and technology, limit and presuppose one another, maintaining a certain tolerable equilibrium. Obviously this balance is extremely unstable. The scales can tip in either direction.

On the one hand the secularized life can become nihilism. For the basis of their peculiar balance of Powers is a disbelief in the deity and the binding authority of any one of them. Should this disbelief get the upper hand, life becomes a spiritual desert. This need not lead to despair; it can be a very heroic attitude. In this position a man has no handhold outside himself. He has "seen through" every claim to authority, every call to obedience coming from outside himself. If he grants to these claims any weight at all, it is only in order that the tolerable equilibrium which gives him breathing space might not break down.

It is always an open question whether man can survive in this nihilism, which is the threatening background and for many, in fact, the very climate of secularized life. The conviction that there is no other choice if he wants to live somehow or other enables him to hold out for a long time in the two postures just described. But they are unnatural postures. Therefore there lurks in men a hankering, usually unconscious, but sometimes suddenly springing into the open, after a "restoration of the Powers," after the secure purposefulness of a life which is placed and is lived under the sign of an inspiring and unifying idea. Fascism and Nazism have proved how near the surface of the European spirit this hankering for authority slumbers. The charm of communism for millions in Europe should not be attributed only to its solutions for social problems, but also, even primarily, to the fact that it is a "political-social world religion." The peoples of Asia, who have undergone but little Christian influence and have lived under the Powers so much longer, feel themselves unable to live without the presence of such a new absolute.

We spoke of a "restoration of the Powers." This is inexact. There is no "return" after the Powers have been unmasked and disarmed by the proclamation of the gospel. Whenever the Powers seek by a counterrevolutionary *coup d'état* to regain their control, they are of necessity something different from what they were before the encounter with Christ. Even in their rebellion the mark of their subjection to the Lord Christ is written on their foreheads. Instead of solid "guardians and trustees" they have become angry anti-Christian usurpers. Their authority is no longer self-evident. They must counter with more powerful means the profound disbelief in their saving virtue, which since Christ lives ineradicable in the human spirit. Propaganda, terror, and the artificial ideologizing of all of life are inseparable concomitants of the rule of the Powers since Christ. We cannot return to the old China or the old Babel. "Who the cup to his lips has once set, his soul now of innocence is bereft."

This is why the restoration of the Powers cannot be a solution. The artificiality and the grimness of their reign robs human life of such essential values that there are still millions of persons for whom the price of their restoration is higher than they are ready to pay. The crisis of our culture is such that men can hold their ground in several ways, none of which, however, leads to a solution in keeping with our nature and purpose. We suffer from "a thirst that can never be slaked at a spring we might find here below."

Is there then besides secularism, nihilism, and "restoration" no fourth solution? Even if we set aside as unrealistic the supposition that more than a small minority among men might belong to the true church of Christ, we must still affirm that there is a fourth possibility. It can happen that Christ's church, by her preaching, her presence, and the patterns of life obtaining within her fellowship, may represent such a mighty witness and so forcefully address the consciences of men far beyond her borders, that they generally orient themselves by this reality, tacitly accepting it as a landmark. They do so because they know of no better guarantor of a decent life, of mercy, freedom, justice, and humanity than a certain general acknowledgment of the sovereignty of Christ, or (as they prefer to say it) of "Christianity" and "Christian values." From one particular point of view this general acceptance is something powerful. It is a weighty positive sign of Christ's dominion over the Powers and of His hold on the conscience; a grasp which also is seen to extend far beyond the borders of the church.

This situation is not only conceivable, beside the other possibilities; it has repeatedly become real and effective, and is still real and effective, in numerous forms of apparently fully secularized behavior. We can label this as a "Christianization" of the Powers. But we must be cautious with the word. It can mean no more than that the Powers, instead of being ideological centers, are what God meant them to be: helps, instruments, giving shape and direction to the genuine life of man as child of God and as neighbor.

That they are "Christianized" means they are made instrumental, made modest; one could even say "neutralized." Provided one keeps clear that all of this is no end in itself (if it were, we would be back in secularism), but oriented by and pointed toward God's dealings with men in Jesus Christ and to men's life in fellowship with this same God. It belongs to the nature of the various

Powers that their "Christianizing" cannot mean the same thing in every case.

For the state it means "de-ideologizing," a reduction to its true dimensions. The state no longer serves its own interest and no longer enslaves men to the world view it propagates; it becomes simply a means of staving off chaos and ordering human relations in such a way that we can lead a quiet and stable life and follow God's call, unhampered by external hindrances.

In the economic and technical realms "Christianizing" will mean the subjection of their resources to serve man as defined by the divine intention. In the educational realm "Christianization" will mean warding off ideologies and offering to children a view of God's redeeming works and of His will for their lives. In law it will mean that legislation and execution will be based on what God in His Word calls good and evil. In one case the relevance of God's revelation is thus nearer and more direct than in another. But in every case the Powers are relativized, made modest. They no longer pretend to offer an inspiring center for all of life. In this world one tacitly assumes that the center is somewhere else, above the Powers, and that life receives its inspiration and its hope from a higher sphere. This awareness, however vague and however unconscious it may be, enables one to bear the fact that the Powers have been dethroned. One understands intuitively that only thus can life's livability be assured.

Such an order of things is not automatic. That it can be a reality, we know in Europe, and not alone from history. This "Christianization" is much more strongly present than we suspect. But the borderline between the "Christianized" and the secularized life is so fluid that no one can say where one ends and the other begins. For "Christianization" is itself a form, indeed the only legitimate form, of secularization. In what we call "secularization" the connection between the Powers and Christ has again been broken and they have regained something of their former position. This is a more "natural" order than "Christianization." The restoration of the Powers would be the most normal arrangement, were it not that since Christ the Powers can only operate in an angry and perverted way, so that their return to power in our society, as prevalent as is the tendency in that direction, will always meet fierce resistance. Within his secularized existence man hankers after a "God or society to harness my being in inspired bonds."[16] But Christ's lordship (what we call "Christian values") is still so much in so many people's blood that they attempt with all their might to escape the chilly grasp of the Powers. Such a pendulum movement is characteristic of a culture above which the name of Christ has been proclaimed. The desperate opposition between America and Russia, between democracy and dictatorship, is a sign thereof.

Such a pendular movement is in one sense normal: "Christianization" is not. A life whose structures and institutions are open on the side of God's revelatory deeds does not come into being automatically. A situation is only thus "open" as long as it is held open by Christ Himself, who conquered the Powers and to whom all authority in heaven and earth is given. For the exercise of this authority He does not need the church; yet it is just as true that He repeatedly chooses to use His church to this end. There is no "objective lordship" without the church, the primary sign of that lordship, in its midst.

Nor can we speak of this lordship apart from the prophetic—to say nothing of the political and organizational—energy which the church brings to bear at a given conjuncture of time. He who believes and is grasped by this lordship knows that its advance will not be without him. That "Christianization" cannot be taken for granted is a constant challenge to the church so to occupy herself, that through the openings which are held open, where there is something to see, the sight may be inspiring. As far as we may know, "Christianization" is inconceivable apart from the prophetic, living testimony of a vital church in word, deed, and presence. Less is too little. To strive to neutralize the Powers and de-ideologize life, without taking as point of departure and as goal the reality of God in Christ, will take us no further than a certain degree of "humanization," which today or tomorrow will fall prey to a new Power, that of "humanity." To strive to neutralize the Powers and de-ideologize life by seeking to shore up the prophetic message with coercive measures, in order thereby to enthrone Christ without passing by the detour of preaching and conversion, will achieve too much and thereby too little. This would but replace one Power by another—in this case by a Christian ideology—whose legalistic character would tend to veil from sight the Lord's salvation and to degenerate into hypocrisy.

The minimum and at the same time the maximum to which we are called is what Paul himself teaches: to be a church which in word and deed lives from the fact that Christ has overcome the Powers, and which holds them at arm's length by virtue of this faith. Then Christ, thanks to His objective sovereignty, will see to it that the very existence of the church will limit and thereby in reality break the hold of the Powers. In this sense the church is ultimately responsible for the contemporary cultural crisis.[17]

A clear example of the exorcising might which the life and witness of the church may exert is the way in which this church, without possessing any strength or taking any action, simply by her refusal to participate in the polytheism and the Caesar-worship of the Roman Empire, put an end to that empire. What was possible then can still be done. Even recent Dutch history gives examples of this on a small scale. The domination of autonomous, enlightened, virtuous man, which liberalism sought to establish a century ago, has been limited and broken (at least partly) because the church stubbornly resisted, especially in the field of education. Similarly democracy, which according to the French precedent was founded on the ideology of popular sovereignty, has been reduced to a set of practical rules to serve human action on the political level.

In addition to the Christian church, the socialistic ideology also helped undermine liberalism. The fact that in this success socialism was willing to deny its ideological character, an event to which Christians within and without the movement contributed decisively, is once again, for those who wish to see it, a sign of Christ's mastery over the Powers which seek to encapsule our lives.[18] It is a saddening sign of the spiritual poverty of much of Netherlands Christianity that many desire only to depreciate or to deprecate this achievement. On the other hand, those who were actively involved therein must be asked if they realize the unspeakable risk which accompanies the end of ideologies. When the spiritual dwelling of thousands of workingmen is empty, more evil spirits enter than had been expelled before. Neutralization without the living prophecy of the church is only the more threatening. Thus we must be deeply grateful to all those who, often abused by orthodox Christians, gave body to this prophecy in word and deed, on the border between church and world.

But the battle with the Powers continues. "Christianized" here, they burst out elsewhere. Each "Christianizing" has only a partial and temporal value. The church's great question is always which Powers are now attempting to get life under their control. This can usually be seen better from a distance. The young churches in the Far East face an imminent struggle with nationalism. They themselves and the peoples among whom they live will have to learn to see and to handle their national existence, not as an end, but as a means to a higher end.

And what of communism? He who believes in Christ's victory cannot believe that the Powers of class and state, which have taken on the form of communism, are invincible. The church which resists in word and deed the ideological poisoning of her life (as she is doing today in the East Zone of Germany) can pray and can expect that Christ will endow with a far-reaching efficacy the encirclement of the Powers which she proclaims. Why then should no communistic society be possible, wherein a totally new economic order fills a purely matter-of-fact role, where the church within an equally practically oriented state system holds her vision of Christ's higher rule intact? The idealist who considers communism harmless misunderstands completely the strength of the Powers. The pessimist who considers communism incorrigible misunderstands completely the lordship of Christ. The living, prophesying Christian church goes her own way despite optimism and pessimism alike.

Then the disciples came to Jesus and said, when they were alone with Him, "Why could we not cast it out?" He said to them, "Because of your little faith. For truly I say to you, if you had faith like a mustard seed, you would say to this mountain, 'move from here to there' and it will move. Nothing shall be impossible to you" (Matthew 17:19 f.).

And He said to them, "This kind cannot be driven out by anything but prayer" (Mark 9:29).

Author's Epilogue

The Significance of Paul's Doctrine of the Powers

The foregoing has made clear that the significance of Paul's view of the Powers should not be sought directly in the domain of theology. Theology occupies itself with who God is according to His revelation and how He deals with us. The Powers belong to human experience, within which God works to preserve, reconcile, and fulfill. They belong thus not so much to Paul's theology as to his view of life and the world.

"World view" is a term no longer in good repute. We sense, rightly, that such a set of ideas, not based directly on revelation, can take on a theological significance and distort Christian faith into a philosophical system. But for Paul this danger does not exist. Not by accident does this study bear the title "Christ and the Powers." We have always to do with Christ and with His saving dealings with the world. For Paul's thought, the Powers serve to express the meaning of Christ's work.

But then there is no excuse not to understand what these Powers signify. Through God's dealings with the world we get a glimpse of how He "views the world." In this sense a certain amount of "world view" is a part of faith. In the light of God's action Paul perceived that mankind is not composed of loose individuals, but that structures, orders, forms of existence, or whatever they be called, are given us as a part of creaturely life and that these are involved, as much as men themselves, in the history of creation, fall, preservation, reconciliation, and consummation. This insight he expressed in the terms and concepts of his time.[19] The insight which is embodied in these terms keeps for us its meaning and validity. We find it expressed all through the Bible. The prophets' campaign against the worship of the forces of nature under the name of Baal, Jesus' warnings about Mammon, the characterization of the absolutist state in Revelation 13, and much of what the New Testament says about demons—to cite only a few examples—encompass the same proclamation which Paul framed in words like "principalities" and "dominions." To observe this is also to demonstrate that we are not bound by Paul's language. Yet I can conceive of readers of these pages who might gratefully adopt not only the insights but also the expressions. In our time the Powers are again more concretely visible than a generation ago; in the same measure we again understand better the words in which Paul clothed his gospel.

Paul can help us with the problems of comparative religions. To see the pre-Christian faiths as a life in subjection to the Powers, following Galatians 4, will preserve us from illegitimate rapprochements with Christian faith (for example, as if it were the "highest form" of religiosity), as well as from an equally illegitimate condemnation of "blind heathendom." Philosophy as well (that is, metaphysics) may be illuminated when we note how many great thinkers have sought to explain the universe on the basis of one or a few Powers. The contribution Paul can make to ethics and to our understanding of political and social life needs no further emphasis after what we observed in our final chapter. Yet our whole exposition is still open to the reproach of having said far too little about the bringing to bear of Paul's preaching on contemporary life. The application and adaptation to our situation would demand another book, which someone else must write. This book has fulfilled its purpose if it helps a broader circle to begin to see the great questions of their own time with the eyes of faith and to discover God's Word as a light on our path even in this realm. It is an appeal to put on the whole armor of God and to wrestle with the evil spirits in the air.

Translator's Epilogue

Professor Berkhof himself has identified (note 19) some of the treatments of the Powers theme by Scripture scholars. He made no effort to survey the broader band of literature which exploits the Powers cosmology and soteriology for new light on contemporary Christian thought and life. Neither can this brief epilogue provide a survey. It is, however, fitting to identify specimens of the wider fruitfulness of Power analysis. Most recent and most thorough is a chapter in Richard Mouw's *Politics and the Biblical Drama* (Eerdmans, 1976), with a view particularly to the possibility of a biblically warranted modern philosophy of politics. Narrower is William Stringfellow's polemic use of the same language, englobed in a wider appropriation of apocalyptic imagery, in his *An Ethic for Christians and Other Aliens in a Strange Land* (Word, 1973). Stringfellow's concern is culture critique, without equal attention to the affirmations of the creaturely dignity of the Powers or of a preserving or saving work of Christ. My own summary in *The Politics of Jesus* (Eerdmans, 1972), little more than an expansion of Berkhof's analysis, was concerned only to demonstrate that the thought of Paul is a compatible expression of (rather than a rejection of) the gospel witness to Jesus, and that it speaks to some of the ways moderns have argued the irrelevance of Jesus to the realm of Power.

Yet by recounting these testimonies to the *relevance* of the Power language we have only begun to test the *faithfulness* of this contemporary interpretation. Some critics, attacking Berkhof in the form of criticism of my *Politics of Jesus*, feel that the affirmation of contemporary relevance illegitimately demythologizes what should be taken as describing a normative cosmology concerned with angelic personalities very hard to reconcile with modernity. On the other hand, the first reaction of Karl Barth (recounted in Berkhof's second preface) was that it was still too "mythological." On the level of "what Paul really meant," critics would want to challenge the disavowal, stated but not argued, of "a conventional orthodox doctrine about angels and devils." On the level of "what Paul really means," the debate remains open. It is a significant service to that continuing debate that the basic introduction by Berkhof is again available.

Notes

1 The biblical texts cited here are drawn from no one English version; of the various phrasings current in contemporary versions those have been chosen which seem nearest to the Dutch (Trans.).

2 Otto Everling, in the introduction to his *Die paulinische Angelologie und Dämonologie*, Göttingen, 1888, remarked that "the utterly subordinate significance of this segment of Paul's thought world seems to have become too generally axiomatic for one to give serious attention to it" (p. 4).

Martin Dibelius' *Die Geisterwelt im Glauben des Paulus*, Göttingen, 1909, was a mature product of the so-called "history of religions" school. In an exemplary piece of scholarship Dibelius placed Paul's expressions in the context of contemporary religious thought. Even today this erudite and carefully written work has not lost its significance. Dibelius rightly sees Paul's uniqueness in his belief that the Powers were conquered in Christ. But he is interested in the Powers themselves only from the viewpoint of comparative religion, since in our time "ideas of spirits and devils" are "in the process of disappearing."

3 First to share this discovery was Heinrich Schlier, in lecture with which he inaugurated his instructorship in Marburg, *Mächte und Gewalten im Neuen Testament* (*Theologische Blätter*, IX/11, Nov. 1930, cols. 289 ff.). Schlier observes that the background of these concep-

tions in comparative religion had been studied, but "we have generally neglected even to ask whether Scripture and Christian tradition might be thinking of definite life experiences when they speak of the devil and the demons, and what experiences might be meant." We hear aright; the Marburg of Heidegger and Bultmann is speaking. Schlier sees in the Powers no objective realities, but projections of what we might call, with Bultmann, man's "self-understanding." This is Schlier's philosophical prejudice, which is open to question. Nevertheless, he did in this way thoughtfully ask about the relevance of Paul's view of the Powers.

In the *Theologische Aufsätze* offered to Karl Barth (Münich, 1936) Günther Dehn published his well-known article, *Engel und Obrigkeit* (pp. 90-106). Noting that in Rom. 13:1 Paul calls the state a "Power," and referring to Dan. 10:13, 20, Dehn saw the Powers as manifested especially in the state. When we think of the date of publication, we realize that this idea belongs to the vision of the confessing church. No wonder that around this interpretation a broad debate arose, in which K. L. Schmid (who had previously pointed in this direction), E. Stauffer, G. Kittel, O. Eck, H. Fuchs, later also K. Barth, Leenhardt, and Cullmann participated. Especially Kittel (*Christus und Imperator*, Stuttgart-Berlin, 1939) opposed Dehn sharply and at length.

It is understandable but regrettable that the problem of the Powers was thus one-sidedly bound up with the political issue, which threatened to lead the biblical-theological investigation into an impasse. It is not said, and certainly not immediately demonstrable, that the very current and ordinary word "powers" in Rom. 13 must be connected with the "Powers" of which Paul speaks in the texts we are now studying. In any case the relationship between the Powers and the world, as we shall further see, is understood by Paul to be far broader, and we can only say something about the state within the broader context. Schmid places the problem in the broader frame in his article, *Die Natur- und Geisteskräfte bei Paulus* (in *Eranos-Jahrbuch*, Zürich, 1947, pp. 87-143). Regrettably, however, this article had little impact because of its weak composition and many digressions. Further notice is due Dr. W. Aalders' *Cultuur en Sacrament* (Nijkerk, 1948), which discusses the angelic powers and the *stoicheia* (cf. below note 6, Aalders' p. 63 ff.) relevantly and in detail. He develops insights which are of great import for the matter at hand. By attending one-sidedly to the positive, preserving functions of the Powers, he, however, comes to untenable conclusions.

Much has been said and written in postwar Germany about the Powers. What has come to my attention has, however, been too much under the impress of postwar attitudes and too little disciplined by exegesis to be of lasting importance.

4 The above-named book by Dibelius has gathered together abundant material in exposition of the background of Paul's thought

in both Jewish and Gentile thought. Likewise Kittel's *Theologisches Wörterbuch zum Neuen Testament* contains references to such material (cf. the articles, *angelos, dynamis, exousia*). Especially *Enoch*, an apocalyptic writing from the first century BC, contains significant parallels to Paul's epistles.

5 This text demonstrates a connection between the Powers and the state, which could not be proved from Rom. 13 alone. The state is but one of the many earthly realities, through which the Powers manifest themselves. (Cf. Oscar Cullmann, *The State in the New Testament*, Scribners, 1956, pp. 50-70, 95-114; and *Christ and Time*, Westminster, 1950, pp. 191-210.)

6 *Stoicheia* is a neuter plural, derived from the root *stoicheioo*, "to stand in a row." A *stoicheion* (neuter singular) is a unit within a row, thence by derivation a letter in an alphabet, a unit in a series of letters or words. Figuratively it can refer to "first principles," "elementary instruction" (as in Heb. 5:12), or to the parts, the "elements" or basic materials of which the world is put together. This usage is very frequent in Greek philosophy, and in the sphere of Hellenistic Judaism (*Wisdom of Solomon* 7:17; 19:18; *IV Maccabees* 12:13); in the New Testament it occurs in 2 Pet. 3:10-12. This is the sense which fits very well, as we shall see, in Paul's line of thought.

But the investigation of comparative religions, both extensive and intensive, has in recent decades led research in another direction. It appears that in the religious usage of Paul's days (thinking especially of Jewish-apocalyptic circles) frequently personal, spiritual beings were designated as *stoicheia*. This would seem to be a quite different meaning from what we noted above. Yet we observed earlier that the world was then thought of as being administered through "angels" (in Jewish thought) or by subordinate gods or "demons" (in Gentile thought). These ruled especially over the forces of nature, among which the stars had a special importance. With this personal aspect we find the "world elements" in the Book of *Enoch* and in *IV Esdras*. There *stoicheia* should be rendered "elemental spirits," "world spirits," or "astral spirits."

Yet in my opinion there are serious reasons to doubt that Paul is following apocalyptic usage, and not the older, more general understanding of *stoicheia* as the elements of nature. Granted, there are arguments for the narrower sense, found not so much in Col. 2 as in the passage yet to be treated, Gal. 4. There they are called "guardians and trustees" (v. 2) or "gods" (v. 8). To serve them is to observe "days, months, seasons, and years" (v. 10). The translation "astral deities" would seem obvious. But when Paul further defines this "guardianship," we are at once outside of the apocalyptic climate. Further, Paul is speaking in Colossians and Galatians not of the rule of the stable powers of nature, but of enslavement to speculation, traditions, dietary laws, holy days, and Israel's law in general. One could suspect the powers of sun, moon, and stars behind the feast days, but for this there is no need. Especially in Galatians, written to Jewish Christians, we have every reason to think of the feast days prescribed by their law. But it is as true of Colossians, where the festivals (including the sabbath), together with dietary rules, are called "a shadow of what was to come" (v. 17). Paul believes that the transition which his readers are likely to make from paganism to the observance of Jewish laws indicates that they still—or again—are living under the *stoicheia.* With reference to their pagan past Paul may be thinking of the worship of astral powers, though this is not certain, but when he sees both Jews and Gentiles under the curse of the *stoicheia,* it is sure that the meaning is far broader, no longer explicable from the apocalyptic background, pointing rather to the older and more general meaning of "basic elements of the world." It is significant that Schlier in his commentary, after decidedly choosing the rendering "astral deities," is unable to make any sense of this definition in his exposition of the passage. He is constantly paraphrasing *stoicheia* in other ways. He writes of "the slavery, in which the world holds man through the law of its elementary essences" (*Wesenheiten,* p. 137); or of "the Kosmos in its elementary forces, in the power of the impressiveness of the events of Nature and of Fate . . . , following the law of the world . . . , the blind apotheosis of the Kosmos . . . , cosmic process in which the autonomous world exalts itself" (p. 143).

The Leiden dissertation, *Stoicheia tou kosmou,* of A. W. Cramer (The Hague, 1961) argues that these terms were not yet used of astral powers in Paul's times. He distinguishes strictly between the Powers and fallen angels (differing with Schlier, to my mind rightly). He likewise denies, on grounds which seem to me weak, the close connection of the *stoicheia* and the Powers; as a result the *stoicheia* are vaguely described only as "the elements of the religious-moral habit of 'old man' " (p. 126).

7 This is especially true of the above-named work of M. Dibelius. He concludes hastily and uncritically that similarity means inner agreement. As a result almost all contemporary theologians feel obliged to connect Paul's "Powers" with *Enoch's* ranks of angels, and consequently have not the least idea what to do theologically with the whole set of ideas. And yet the comparative method—on condition that it be used descriptively and not superficially or with presuppositions of causality—is the most helpful means of finding and illuminating in a scientific way what is central and original in the biblical proclamation.

8 Usually the discussion of the Powers as angels has been limited to a citation of Col. 1:16 as proof of their existence and their subjection to Christ. We smile to learn how the conclusion is drawn from Eph.

3:10 that angel's knowledge is based on experience and capable of being propagated. (Heppe, *Reformed Dogmatics*, London, 1950, p, 205 f. Similar statements can be found in the classical dogmatic works of Bavinck and H. Schmidt.)

More recent systematic theology texts (cf. those of Althaus, Brunner, Elert, Vogel) yield nothing essentially new. The only theologian who to my knowledge has noticed the problems which arise here is Karl Barth, who in his *Church Dogmatics* (Vol. III/3) devotes to Paul's view of the Powers a few pages of his long discussion of angels. In addition to the political sense of "Power" Barth distinguishes two uses of the world, namely, for *heavenly* and for *demonic* powers. In the first category fall "the powers of order, . . . salutary forces for the establishment of a relative peace, the relative aversion of chaos and therefore in this sense the furtherance of the kingdom of God" (p. 458).

On the basis of 1 Cor. 15:24 Barth considers himself obliged to conceive these powers as temporal. He views the demonic powers as competitors and mimics of the heavenly powers. Evidently, Barth has seen something essential; yet it is just as evident that his construction is very forced (using the same name for two opposing kinds of beings in 1 Cor. 15:24, related to good angels whose work is brought to an end). The fact that Barth, with all other theologians before him, understands the Powers as angels drove him to the artifice of two classes of powers—all the more because contrary to his predecessors, he considers an angelic fall to be unthinkable (*ibid.*, p. 622 f.). Meanwhile most theologians have not even dealt with the problem; they felt that the biblical description of angels and Paul's statements about the Powers were not to be reconciled.

9 In Luke 7:24 and 9:52 and Jas. 2:25 *angelos* means ordinary human messengers. In Matt. 11:10 John the Baptist is thus designated. Cf. Kittel's *Theol. Wörterbuch* and Dibelius, *op. cit.*, who concludes, "by no means need we always connect *angelos* in the New Testament with the *ml'kim* of the Old, for in Jesus' time paganism had its own demonological meaning of *angelos.*" These pagan "angels" were chthonic beings, i.e., personified forces of nature.

10 Paul's positive evaluation of God's goodness as mediated in life under the Powers shines through the reports of two of his missionary sermons: in Acts 14:16 ff. and 17:26-30. Remarkably, according to the sense of Gal. 4:1-10 in its context, Paul thinks of Jewish law as also such a world power to which men are enslaved. This need not surprise us when we remember that this is just one of the facets of Paul's view of the law. He is thinking not of the law as intended by God to lead to Christ, nor (still less) of love as the "law of Christ," but of a system of external religious, ethical, cultic, and social rules which were thought to be the essential, humanly fulfillable will of God. The law thus

conceived was no longer an expression of God's intention, yet still served as the framework of Jewish society.

11 In his article (cited above, note 3) K. L. Schmidt attempted to illuminate the nature of the Powers by beginning with the concept "name." He reminds us of the binding and conjuring power of the name "as a demonic entity in its force and antiforce. The lying power of evil propaganda is thus a segment of this whole realm of spiritual powers . . ." (p. 140). If this is properly stated (Smith exemplifies it with Hitler's own language, p. 138 ff.), then it is quite significant that for Paul the "name," beside the other Powers, exercises a function in the glorified creation.

12 *Church Dogmatics*, Vol. II/2, pp. 662 ff.

13 Paul expresses this powerfully in 1 Cor. 3. The names of Peter, Apollos, and his own came for many to be ideologies or Powers, by which they oriented their belief and life. They said, "I am Paul's" or "I am of Apollos" (v. 4). Paul reverses the genitive: "You are Christ's (v. 23) and therefore Paul, Apollos, and Peter, yea, world, life, death, present and future are yours" (v. 22).

14 Both of the terms in this title are used with meanings distinct from ordinary American usage. "Crisis" was a major theme in European Protestant theology 1925-45. The other word is the Dutch equivalent of "christening," but that is not what Berkhof means either. We indicate this difficulty of definition by keeping the term in quotation marks in the text. Berkhof has indicated in his second preface that he would no longer use the term. The chapter itself will furnish the best definition of both terms.

15 Marsman, *Tempel en Kruis*, XL.

16 Marsman.

17 Jesus Himself described clearly the situation sketched above in the word which we find in Matt. 12:43-45 and Luke 11:24-26. The context in which Luke reports it is also significant. The nature and the basis of Jesus' exorcisms were being discussed. He calls this a combat against Satan, in which He designates Himself the Victor. But then He warns His hearers not to fix their attention on the exorcisms themselves. They are but the obverse of what really matters. To drive out evil spirits in itself does no good; in fact, it is a highly dangerous business. If a man's dwelling remains empty after its having been purified, this has the greatest attraction for the evil spirits, which can then return in greater numbers. Christ's conquest of the Powers can be blessing or curse; there is no third choice. Secularized life calls for

the restoration of the Powers; a restoration which, however, is no repetition, but greater tyranny. "For this man the last state shall be worse than the first." Only where the presence of the Victor Himself seals the victory, preventing life from remaining empty, is the expulsion of the Powers a blessing.

18 "Liberalism" is here used in a sense proper to European social history, to refer to a humanistic, individualistic, laissez-faire view of social goals (Trans.).

19 The professional interpreters of the New Testament are on the whole more interested in determining which usage Paul made of what material, than in the relevance of his original usage for the present time. If they do move toward the issues of contemporary application, I feel that they are either somewhat arbitrary or too much influenced by recent philosophies or social theories. With this restriction I mention as a further help to understand Paul's meaning:

A. J. Bandstra, *The Law and the Elements of the World: An Exegetical Study in Aspects of Paul's Teaching*, Kampen (Neth.), 1964.

G. B. Caird, *Principalities and Powers*, Oxford, 1956.

H. J. Gabathuler, *Jesus Christus—Haupt der Kirche—Haupt der Welt—Der Christus hymnus Colosser 1, 15-20 in der theologischen Forschung der letzten 130 Jahre*, Zürich and Stuttgart, 1965.

N. Kehl, *Der Christushymnus im Kolosser brief*, Stuttgart, 1967.

G. H. C. MacGregor, *Principalities and Powers: The Cosmic Background of Paul's Thought* in New Testament Studies I (1954-1955), pp. 17-28.

H. Schlier, *Principalities and Powers in the New Testament*, New York, 1961.

Other books deal with our subject from a more dogmatic, philosophical, sociological, or topical viewpoint. I mention three of them, with which I feel a certain degree of congeniality and which may be helpful to my readers for a further development of their thoughts in this field:

E. Gordon Rupp, *Principalities and Powers: Studies in the Christian Conflict in History*, London, 1952. In spite of the title, the powers play a subordinate role; the book's real subject is the Christian concept of history. Rupp's idea of the powers is close to that of my study, as may be seen in his modernization of the old Cornish prayer:

"From 'Anities and 'Alities
and 'Ologies and 'Isms,'
Good Lord, deliver us" (p. 15).

Otto A. Dilschneider, *Christus Pantokrator*, Berlin, 1962, especially pp. 49-97. The subtitle reads: "Vom Kolosserbrief zur Okumene." This book is a profound attempt to interpret in contemporary terms the message of the letters to the Colossians and the Ephesians. It stresses particularly the unity of old mythologies and present ideologies. He deals also, as my book does not, with the influence of the powers within the church (e.g., in the shape of Confessionalism).

A. W. Kist, *Antwoord aan de machten* ("Answer to the Powers"), Alphen aan den Rijn, 1971. This Dutch work follows the lines of my book, enlarged with much recent material, and connects Paul's concept with modern sociology of institutions. The intent is to set new ideals for Christian adult education. The subtitle reads: "Adult Education Work, Viewed from a Socio-Theological Angle."